Fun Chinese Characters 1
快乐汉字

Ping Xu Moroney 许平

Copyright © 2014 Ping Xu Moroney
All rights reserved.
ISBN: 978-0-9906656-0-1

To mom 李秀珍 Lǐ, Xiù Zhēn, *husband John, children Sean* 许杰 Xǔ Jié, *Anne* 许娜 Xǔ nà *and William* 许明 Xǔ míng

CONTENTS

大多数的人觉得学汉字是一件很难又枯草的事，因为要把汉字学好的确不是容易。但汉字是五千年来我们祖先智慧的结晶，也是世界上最古老的文字之一。汉字的魅力是形象字潜藏着丰富的审美和诗意，我们中国文化的骄傲。我们可以用图画把汉字学得快乐，容易。这适合所有的年龄和国籍的学生。通过图片把枯草，我们能把复杂的汉字转变成趣味生动的图画，让更多的人喜爱，欣赏中国的古老汉字的奇特魅力。

Most people think learning Chinese characters is difficult and hard. It can be. However, it is very rewarding as Chinese characters are the crystallization of the wisdom of Chinese ancestors. Developed over the past five thousand years, it is one of the world's most ancient texts. The key to reading Chinese is in decoding the charm of Chinese characters as the image of the word lurks in a wealth of aesthetics and poetry. With practice you can learn to see the images embedded in the characters; when this happens, reading Chinese becomes fun and easy. This approach is suitable for students of all ages and nationalities. The pictures transfer the process of learning, boring and complex, into excitement and animation. This approach to learning allows more people to love and appreciate the unique magic of the ancient Chinese characters.

CHAPTER 1 NUMBER 数字

1 一 One 2 二 Two 3 三 Three 4 四 Four 5 五 Five 6 六 Six 7 七 Seven 8 八 Eight 9 九 Nine 10 十 Ten

CHAPTER 2 SIZE AND DIRECTION 尺寸和方向

11 大 Big 12 中 Middle 13 小 Small 14 上 Above 15 下 Under 16 卡 Stuck

CHAPTER 3 NATURE 自然

17 日 Sun 18 月 Moon 19 明 Bright 20 晶 Crystal 21 火 Fire 22 炎 Flame 23 焱 Flames 24 水 Water 25 川 River 26 雨 Rain 27 云 Cloud 28 气 Gas 29 田 Field 30 金 Gold 31 木 Tree 32 林 Wood 33 森 Forest 34 竹 Bamboo 35 本 Root 36 焚 Burn

CHAPTER 4 BODY 身体

37 目 Eye 38 手 Hand 39 看 Look 40 眉 Eyebrow 41 耳 Ear 42 口 Mouth

CHAPTER 5 MAN 人

43 品 Taste 44 言 Speak 45 心 Heart 46 吕 Surname 47 子 Child 48 女 Woman 49 父 Father 50 母 Mother 51 哭 Cry 52 吃 Eat 53 包 Wrap 54 走 Walk 55 人 Person 56 从 Follow 57 众 People 58 渔 Fishing 59 囚 Prisoner 60 州 State

CHAPTER 6 FOOD 食物

61 瓜 Melon 62 肉 Meat 63 贝 Shell 64 米 Rice 65 禾 Grain

CHAPTER 7 ANIMAL 动物

66 牛 Cow 67 囚 Prison 68 马 Horse 69 鱼 Fish 70 鸟 Bird 71 羊 Sheep 72 鸡 Chicken 73 蛇 Snake 74 鼠 Mouse 75 虎 Tiger 76 兔 Rabbit 77 龙 Dragon

CHAPTER 8 TIME AND ADJECTIVE 时间和形容词

78 春 Spring 79 夏 Summer 80 秋 Autumn 81 冬 Winter 82 易 Easy 83 旦 Dawn 84 早 Early 85 久 Long 86 寒 Cold 87 富 Rich 88 昌 Thriving 89 好 Good 90 安 Save 91 旧 Old 92 灾 Disaster

CHAPTER 9 BUILDING AND OBJECT 建筑和物件

93 门 Door 94 刀 Knife 95 网 Net 96 家 Home 97 字 Word

CHAPTER 10 TRAFFIC 交通

98 乡 Village 99 车 Car 100 止 Stop

Fun Chinese Characters 1 快乐汉字 1

1 一 Yī One

2 二 Èr Two

3 三 Sān Three

4 四 Sì Four

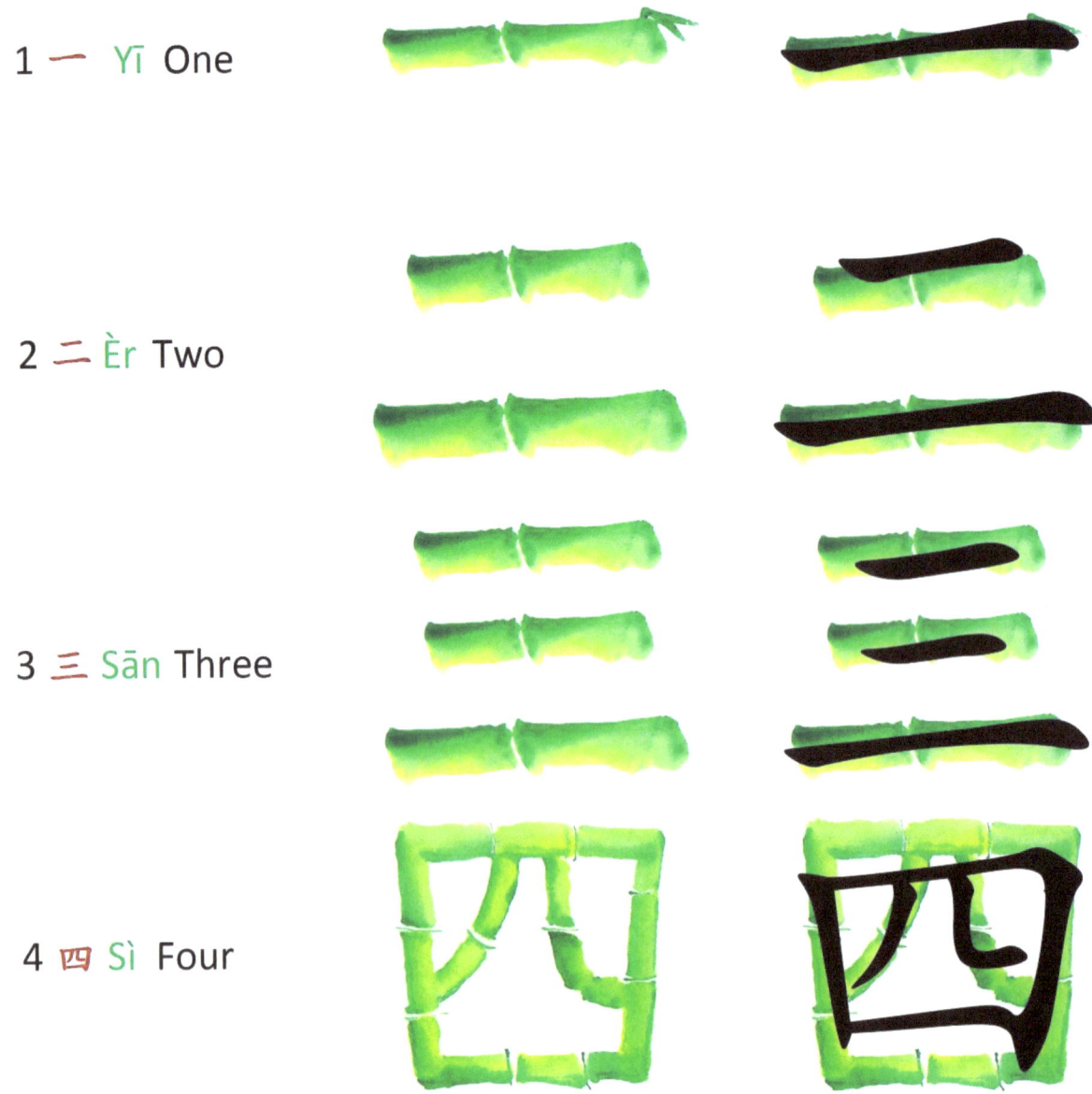

5 五 Wǔ Five

6 六 Liù Six

7 七 Qī Seven

8 八 Bā Eight

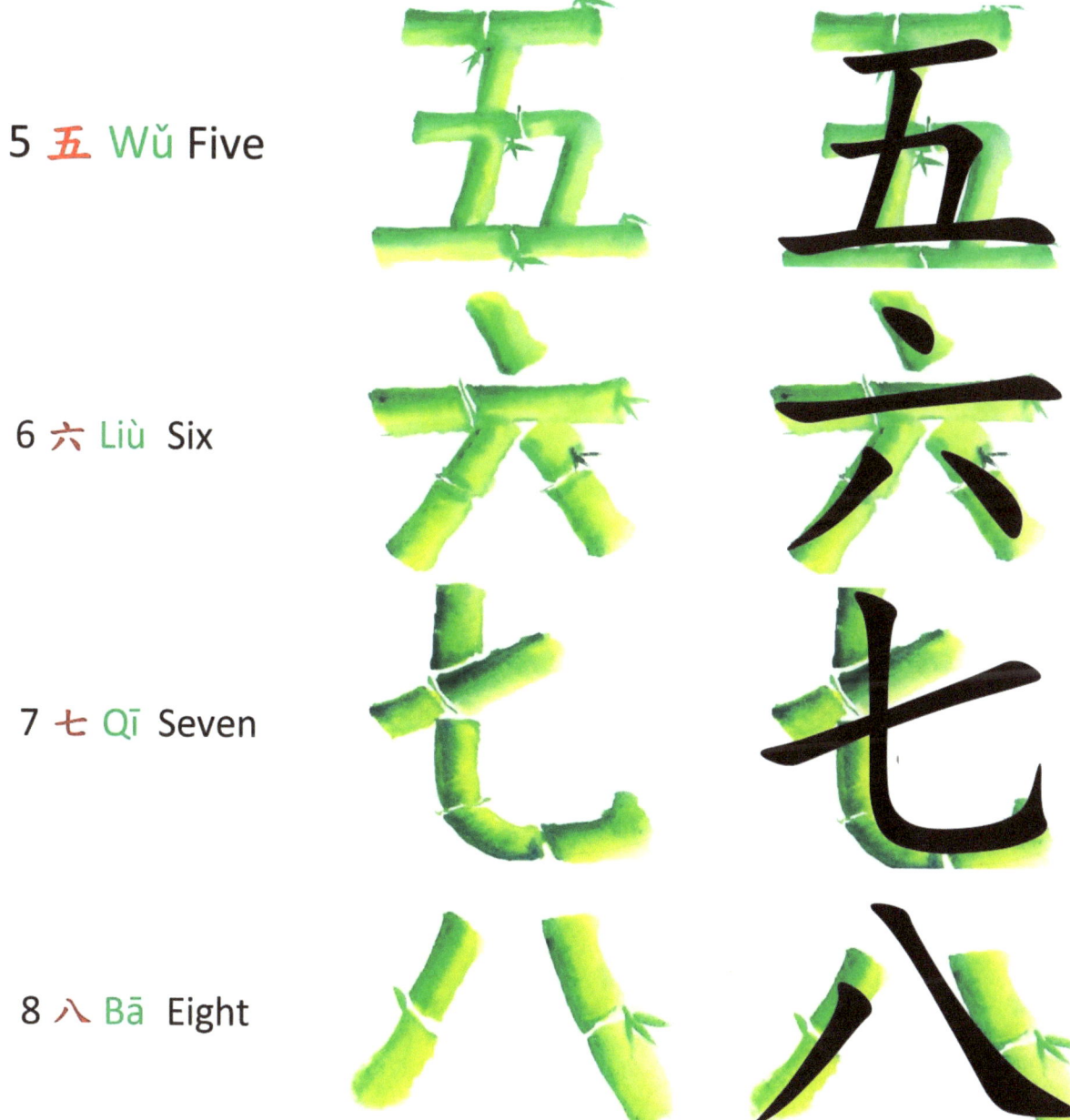

9 九 Jiǔ Nine

10 十 Shí Ten

11 大 Dà Big

12 中 Zhōng Middle

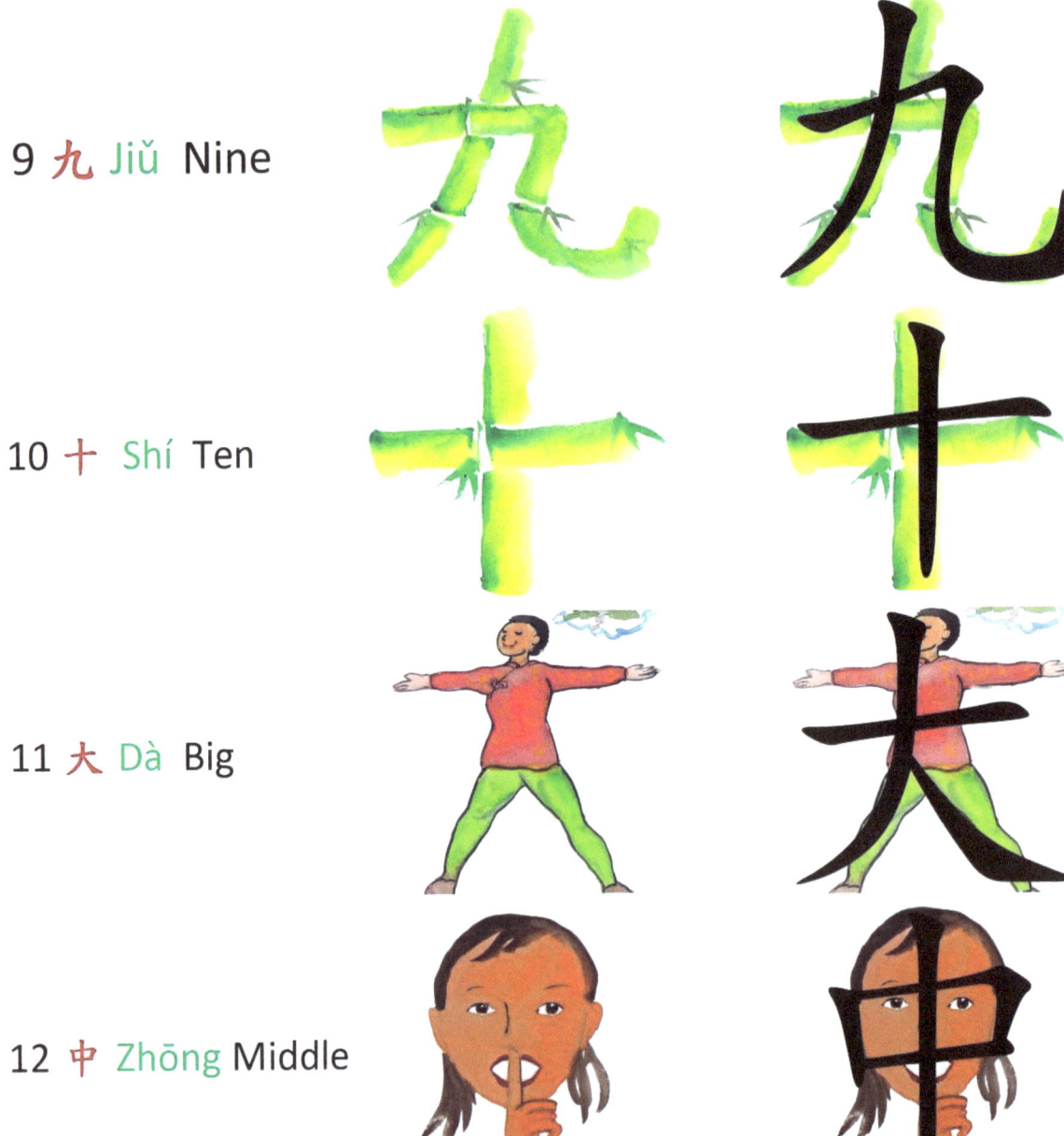

13 小 Xiǎo Small

14 上 Shàng Above

15 下 Xià Down

16 卡 Kǎ Stuck

17 日 Rì Sun

18 月 Yuè Moon

19 明 Míng Bright

20 晶 Jīng Crystal

21 火 Huǒ Fire

22 炎 Yán Flame

23 焱 Yàn Flames

24 水 Shuǐ Water

25 川 Chuān River

26 雨 Yǔ Rain

27 云 Yún Cloud

28 气 Qì Gas

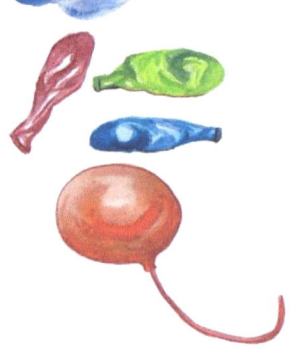 

29 田 Tián Soil

30 金 Jīn Gold

31 木 Mù Tree

32 林 Lín Wood

33 森 Sēn Forest

34 竹 Zhú Bamboo

35 本 Běn Root

36 焚 Fén Burn

37 目 Mù Eye

38 手 Shǒu Hand

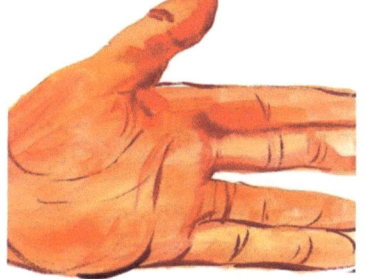 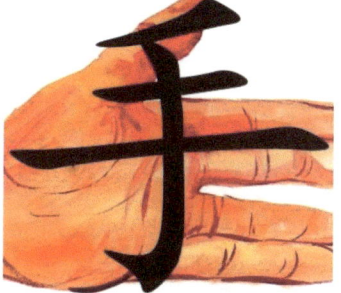

39 看 Kàn Look

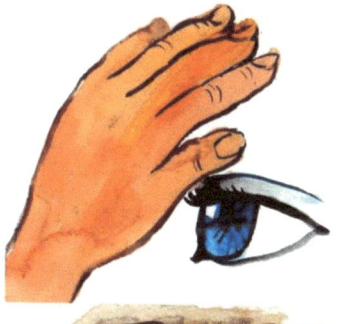 

40 眉 Méi Eyebrow

41 耳 Ěr Ear

42 口 Kǒu Mouth

43 品 Pǐn Taste

44 言 Yán Speak

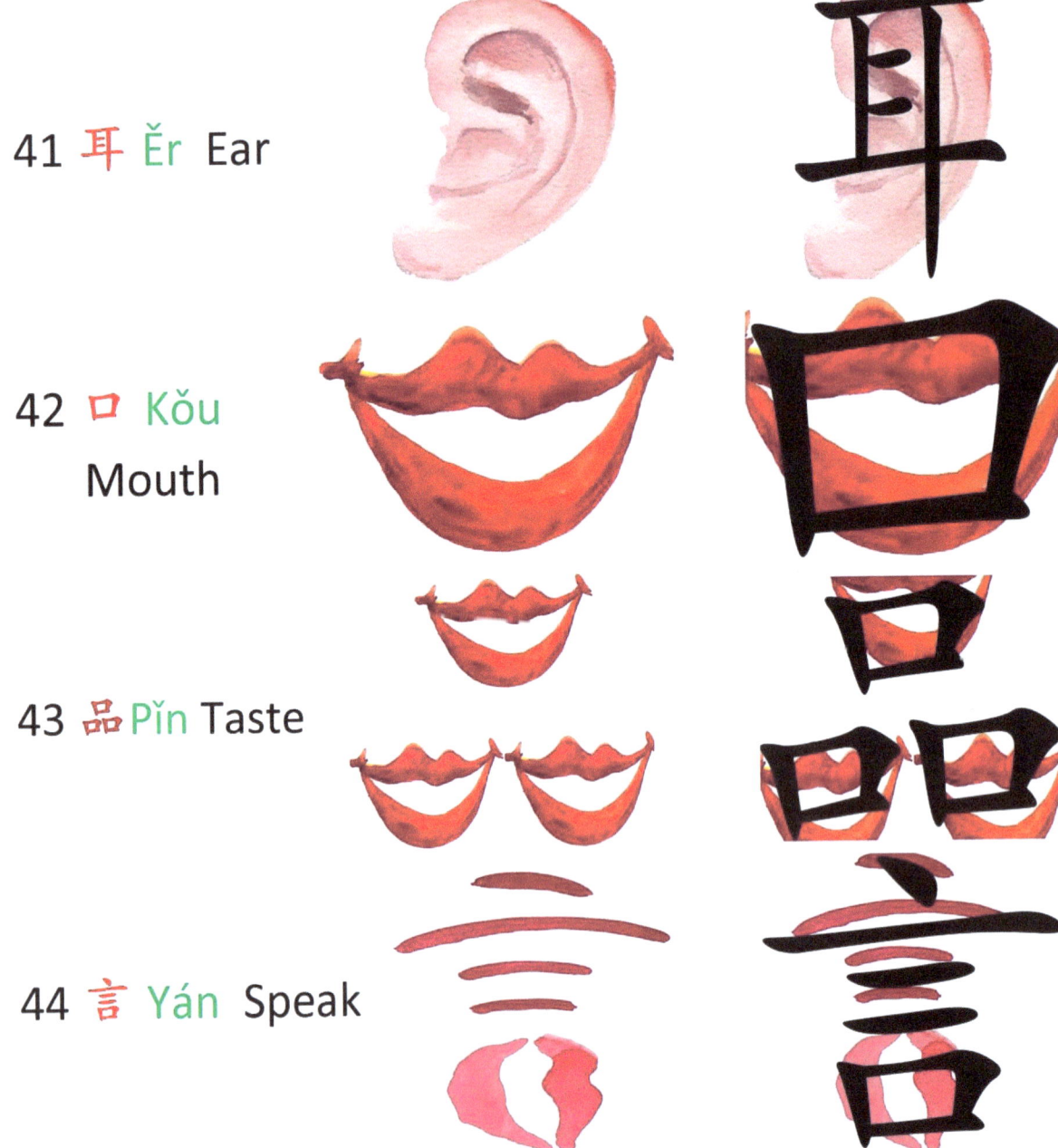

Fun Chinese Characters 1 快乐汉字 1

45 心 Xīn Heart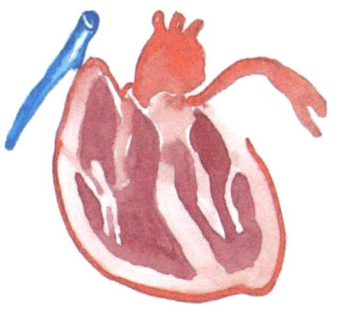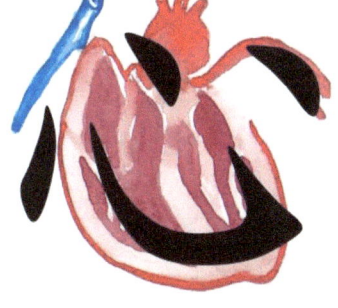

46 吕 lǚ Surname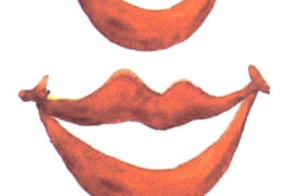

47 子 Zǐ Child

48 女 Nǚ Woman

49 父 Fù Father

50 母 Mǔ Mother

51 哭 Kū Cry

52 吃 Chī Eat

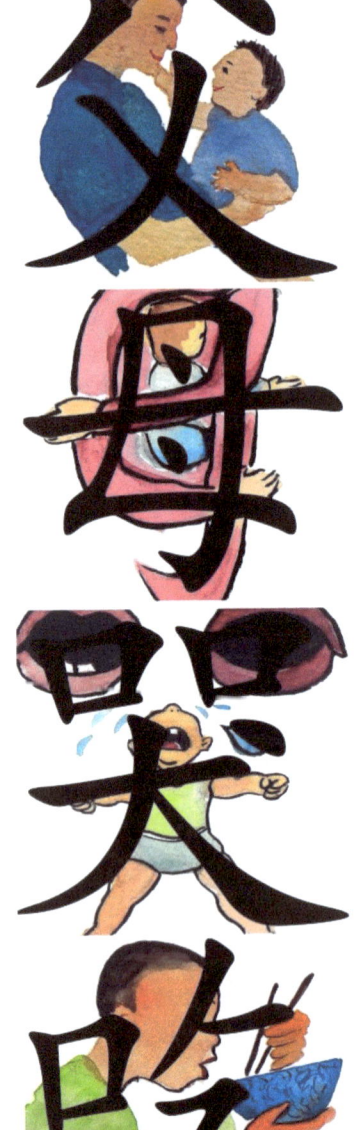

53 包 Bāo Wrap

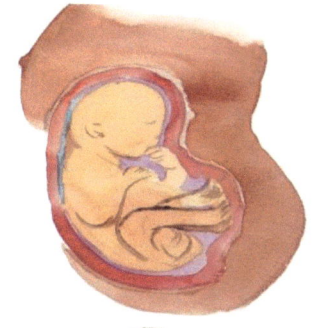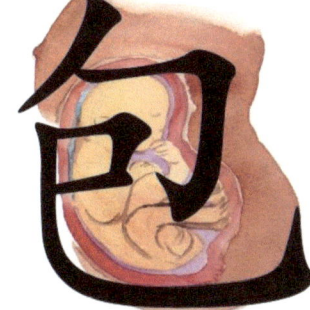

54 走 Zǒu Walk

55 人 Rén Person

56 从 Cóng Follow

57 众 Zhòng
People

58 囚 Qiú Prisoner

59 州 Zhōu State

60 渔 Yú Fishing

61 瓜 Guā Melon

62 肉 Ròu Meat

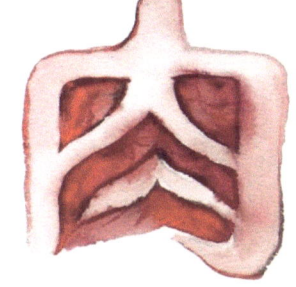 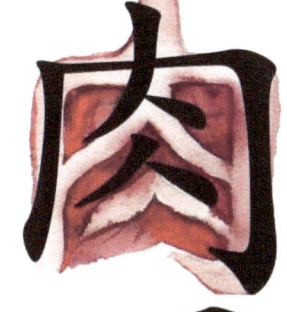

63 贝 Bèi Shell

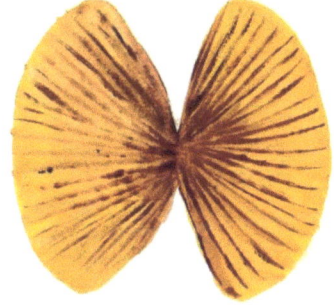 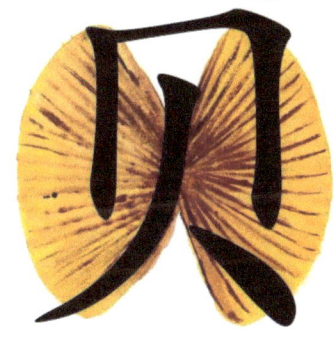

64 米 Mǐ Rice

65 禾 Hé Grain

66 牛 Niú Cow

67 牢 Láo Prison

68 马 Mǎ Horse

69 鱼 Yú Fish

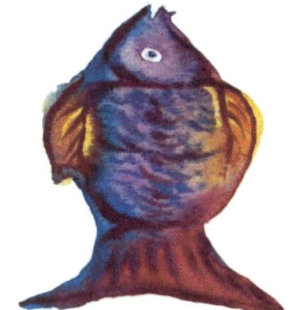 

70 鸟 Niǎo Bird

71 羊 Yáng Sheep

72 鸡 Jī Chicken

73 蛇 Shé Snake

74 鼠 Shǔ Mouse

75 虎 Hǔ Tiger

76 兔 Tù Rabbit

77 龙 Lóng Dragon

78 春 Chūn Spring

79 夏 Xià Sumer

80 秋 Qiū Autumn

81 冬 Dōng Winter

82 易 Yì Easy

83 旦 Dàn Dawn

84 早 Zǎo Morning

85 久 Jiǔ Long

86 寒 Hán Cold

87 富 Fù Rich

88 昌 Chāng Thriving

89 好 Hǎo Good

90 安 Ān Safe

91 旧 Jiù Old

92 灾 Zāi Disaster

93 门 Mén Door

94 刀 Dāo Knife

95 网 Wǎng Net

96 家 Jiā Home

97 字 Zì Character

98 乡 Xiāng Village

99 车 Chē Car

100 止 Zhǐ Stop

ABOUT THE AUTHOR

Ping Xu Moroney 许平

www.pingsgallery.com pingsgallery@aol.com

Ping Xu Moroney was born and studied Chinese art in Shanghai China. She holds a Bachelor's degree in secondary education from Shanghai Teachers Advanced College, a bachelor's degree in International Studies from Kyoritsu Women's University in Japan, a Master's degree in Studio Arts from The College of New Rochelle, and a teaching certificate in Chinese from William Paterson University. She has experience teaching art, Chinese, Japanese and Asian culture subjects in private and public schools in NJ and NY. As a professional artist, she has exhibited and sold fine art paintings through art dealers, galleries and art exhibits in China, Japan and America.

许平出生在上海，自幼学中国画，上海第四师范学校毕业后留学日本。1999 年获日本共立女子大学国际关系学士学位。后移居美国，2003 年获新罗谢尔学院硕士学位。她的作品在市政厅，公共图书馆和其他博物馆多有展示，收藏。2010 年完成威廉-帕特森大学"汉语教师培养项目"的学习，现已获得新泽西州终身汉语和美术教师资格证书。她已有多年在纽约和新泽西州公立和私立学校教学经验。

DEDICATION

I could not have completed the Fun Chinese Characters book one without Dr. Lan Jiang and Dr Ming Jian of William Paterson University. I would like to express a special thanks to all the students and colleges I was fortunate to work with at the Storm King School, Sparta Middle school and Orange County Chinese Language School.

www.ingramcontent.com/pod-product-compliance
Lightning Source LLC
Chambersburg PA
CBHW040020050426
42452CB00002B/67